FOR:_____

*T*he joy of the Lord is your strength.
Nehemiah 8:10

FROM: _____

Promises of Joy for a Woman of Faith
Copyright © 1997 by New Life Clinics
ISBN 0-310-97389-9

Published in association with the literary agency of Wolgemuth & Hyatt, Inc., 8012 Brooks Chapel Rd., #243. Brentwood, Tennessee, 37027.

Requests for information should be addressed to: ZondervanPublishingHouse
Mail Drop B20
Grand Rapids, Michigan 49530
http://www.zondervan.com

Editorial Director: Joy Marple
Project Editor: Mary Pielenz Hampton
Production Editor: Pat Matuszak
Creative Design: Paula Gibson

98 99 00 /HK/ 8

Printed in China

PROMISES OF JOY FOR A WOMAN OF FAITH

Zondervan Gifts
We have a gift for inspiration™

Promises of Joy for a Woman of Faith

on

Creation and God's Wonderful Works
Home and Family
Friends and Fellowship
Our Work and Service
Wisdom, Righteousness and a Pure Heart
God's Plan and His Purpose
Our Savior and Salvation
God's Provision and Protection
God's Word and Worship
God's Comfort and Unfailing Love
God's Presence and the Promise of Eternity

*R*ejoice in the Lord always. I will
say it again: Rejoice.

Philippians 4:4

❧

*T*hroughout Scripture, this is the most often given exhortation. Although at first glance it seems repetitive, a closer look reveals that God brings joy into our lives in many different ways. There are just as many ways to express that joy. The encouragement to rejoice is not just a command to feel glad or be happy. Rejoicing is an act. If we are to truly rejoice as God desires, we must find a way to express that feeling.

The following scripture verses highlight some ways God brings joy into our lives. Many of them also offer suggestions on how to express that joy. We can look at these verses with the view that these same opportunities for rejoicing are still part of our lives today. Some of the passages have been produced as songs that will be familiar to you—stop and sing them. If a passage suggests a certain way to praise the Lord, pause and praise him.

May these pages bring you a new awareness of the tremendous blessings of joy that God has given us and offer new expressions of rejoicing with and before him.

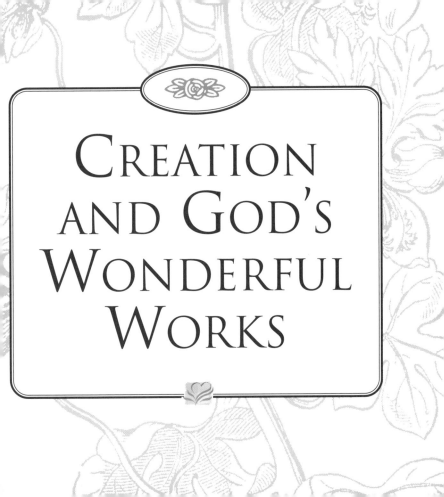

CREATION AND GOD'S WONDERFUL WORKS

*T*his is the day the LORD has made;
let us rejoice and be glad in it.

Psalm 118:24

*H*ow many are your works, O LORD!
In wisdom you made them all; the earth
is full of your creatures.

Psalm 104:24

*B*ut be glad and rejoice forever in what
I will create, for I will create Jerusalem to be
a delight and its people a joy.

Isaiah 65:18

*T*he heavens declare the glory of God;
the skies proclaim the work of his hands.

Psalm 19:1

*M*any, O LORD my God, are the wonders you
have done. The things you planned for us no one
can recount to you; were I to speak and tell of
them, they would be too many to declare.

Psalm 40:5

I praise you because I am fearfully and
wonderfully made; your works are wonderful,
I know that full well.

Psalm 139:14

I will praise you, O Lord, with all my heart;
I will tell of all your wonders. I will be glad
and rejoice in you; I will sing praise to your
name, O Most High.

Psalm 9:1–2

*W*orship the Lord with gladness; come before
him with joyful songs. Know that the Lord is
God. It is he who made us, and we are his; we are
his people, the sheep of his pasture.

Psalm 100:2–3

*M*ay the glory of the L*ord* endure forever;
may the L*ord* rejoice in his works—he who looks
at the earth, and it trembles, who touches
the mountains, and they smoke.

Psalm 104:31–32

❧

*R*emember to extol God's work, which
men have praised in song.

Job 36:24

❧

*F*or you make me glad by your deeds, O L*ord*;
I sing for joy at the works of your hands.
How great are your works, O L*ord*, how
profound your thoughts!

Psalm 92:4-5

O LORD, you are my God; I will exalt you and praise your name, for in perfect faithfulness you have done marvelous things, things planned long ago.

Isaiah 25:1

❧

For since the creation of the world God's invisible qualities—his eternal power and divine nature—have been clearly seen, being understood from what has been made.

Romans 1:20

Our mouths were filled with laughter, our tongues with songs of joy. Then it was said among the nations, "The LORD has done great things for them." The LORD has done great things for us, and we are filled with joy.

Psalm 126:2–3

❧

My lips will shout for joy when I sing praise to you—I, whom you have redeemed. My tongue will tell of your righteous acts all day long.

Psalm 71:23–24

*S*ing to him, sing praise to him; tell of all his wonderful acts. Glory in his holy name; let the hearts of those who seek the LORD rejoice.

1 Chronicles 16:9–10

❧

*S*ing to God, sing praise to his name, extol him who rides on the clouds—his name is the LORD—and rejoice before him.

Psalm 68:4

HOME AND FAMILY

*B*ut if serving the L<small>ORD</small> seems undesirable to you, then choose for yourselves this day whom you will serve, . . . But as for me and my household, we will serve the L<small>ORD</small>.

Joshua 24:15

*R*ejoice in all the good things the L<small>ORD</small> your God has given to you and your household.

Deuteronomy 26:11

*T*hey replied, "Believe in the Lord Jesus, and you will be saved—you and your household."

Acts 16:31

A wife of noble character who can find? She is worth far more than rubies. Her husband has full confidence in her and lacks nothing of value.

Proverbs 31:10-11

*H*er husband is respected at the city gate, where he takes his seat among the elders of the land. She is clothed with strength and dignity; she can laugh at the days to come. She speaks with wisdom, and faithful instruction is on her tongue.

Proverbs 31:23, 25-26

*H*er children arise and call her blessed; her husband also, and he praises her: "Many women do noble things, but you surpass them all." Charm is deceptive, and beauty is fleeting; but a woman who fears the LORD is to be praised. Give her the reward she has earned, and let her works bring her praise at the city gate.

Proverbs 31:28-31

*G*od settles the barren woman in her home as a happy mother of children. Praise the LORD.

Psalm 113:9

❧

*J*esus said, "Let the little children come to me, and do not hinder them, for the kingdom of heaven belongs to such as these."

Matthew 19:14

❧

*B*ut from everlasting to everlasting the LORD's love is with those who fear him, and his righteousness with their children's children.

Psalm 103:17

*T*he fruit of your womb will be blessed,
and the crops of your land and the young
of your livestock— the calves of your herds
and the lambs of your flocks.

Deuteronomy 28:4

❧

*M*ay the LORD make you increase, both you
and your children. May you be blessed by the
LORD, the Maker of heaven and earth.

Psalm 115:14–15

*M*y son, if your heart is wise, then
my heart will be glad; my inmost being will
rejoice when your lips speak what is right.

Proverbs 23:15–16

I have no greater joy than to hear that my
children are walking in the truth.

3 John 1:4

*B*y wisdom a house is built, and
through understanding it is established;
through knowledge its rooms are filled
with rare and beautiful treasures.

Proverbs 24:3-4

*T*he father of a righteous man has great joy;
he who has a wise son delights in him.
May your father and mother be glad;
may she who gave you birth rejoice!

Proverbs 23:24–25

I prayed for this child, and the Lord has
granted me what I asked of him.

1 Samuel 1:27

FRIENDS
AND
FELLOWSHIP

$\mathscr{P}$erfume and incense bring joy to the heart,
and the pleasantness of one's friend springs
from his earnest counsel.

Proverbs 27:9

$\mathscr{I}$ have great confidence in you; I take
great pride in you. I am greatly encouraged;
my joy knows no bounds.

2 Corinthians 7:4

$\mathscr{I}$ always thank my God as I remember you
in my prayers. Your love has given me great joy
and encouragement, because you, brother, have
refreshed the hearts of the saints.

Philemon 1:4,7

$\mathcal{B}$e devoted to one another in brotherly
love. Honor one another above yourselves.
Never be lacking in zeal, but keep your spiritual
fervor, serving the Lord. Be joyful in hope,
patient in affliction, faithful in prayer.

Romans 12:10–12

*M*y intercessor is my friend as my
eyes pour out tears to God.
Job 16:20

A friend loves at all times.
Proverbs 17:17

*T*hose who love a pure heart and are gracious in
speech will have the king as a friend.
Proverbs 22:11 (NRSV)

*T*herefore, my brothers, you whom
I love and long for, my joy and crown,
stand firm in the Lord!

Philippians 4:1

❧

*R*ecalling your tears, I long to see you,
so that I may be filled with joy.

2 Timothy 1:4

*F*or what is our hope, our joy, or the crown in which we will glory in the presence of our Lord Jesus when he comes? Is it not you? Indeed, you are our glory and joy.

1 Thessalonians 2:19–20

*H*ow can we thank God enough for you in return for all the joy we have in the presence of our God because of you?

1 Thessalonians 3:9

Our Work
and Service

*B*lessed are all who fear the LORD, who walk in his ways. You will eat the fruit of your labor; blessings and prosperity will be yours.

Psalm 128:1–2

❧

I know that there is nothing better for men than to be happy and do good while they live. That everyone may eat and drink, and find satisfaction in all his toil—this is the gift of God.

Ecclesiastes 3:12–13

$\mathcal{L}$ikewise all to whom God gives wealth and possessions and whom he enables to enjoy them, and to accept their lot and find enjoyment in their toil—this is the gift of God. For they will scarcely brood over the days of their lives, because God keeps them occupied with the joy of their hearts.

Ecclesiastes 5:19–20 (NRSV)

❧

$\mathcal{G}$ive generously to God and do so without a grudging heart; then because of this the LORD your God will bless you in all your work and in everything you put your hand to.

Deuteronomy 15:10

*Y*ou will be made rich in every way so that you can be generous on every occasion, and through us your generosity will result in thanksgiving to God. This service that you perform is not only supplying the needs of God's people but is also overflowing in many expressions of thanks to God.

2 Corinthians 9:11–12

❧

*S*ix days you shall labor and do all your work, but the seventh day is a Sabbath to the LORD your God.

Deuteronomy 5:13,14

*T*he LORD your God will bless you in all
your harvest and in all the work of your hands,
and your joy will be complete.

Deuteronomy 16:15

❧

*M*ay the favor of the Lord our God rest
upon us; establish the work of our hands for us—
yes, establish the work of our hands.

Psalm 90:17

*M*ake my joy complete by being
like-minded, having the same love, being
one in spirit and purpose.

Philippians 2:2

*Y*our attitude should be the same as that
of Christ Jesus: Who, being in very nature God,
did not consider equality with God something
to be grasped, but made himself nothing,
taking the very nature of a servant, being
made in human likeness.

Philippians 2:5-7

I thank Christ Jesus our Lord, who has given me strength, that he considered me faithful, appointing me to his service.

1 Timothy 1:12

❧

S erve the LORD with fear and rejoice with trembling.

Psalm 2:11

❧

B lessed is he who is kind to the needy.

Proverbs 14:21

*I*f anyone speaks, he should do it as one speaking the very words of God. If anyone serves, he should do it with the strength God provides, so that in all things God may be praised through Jesus Christ. To him be the glory and the power for ever and ever. Amen.

1 Peter 4:11

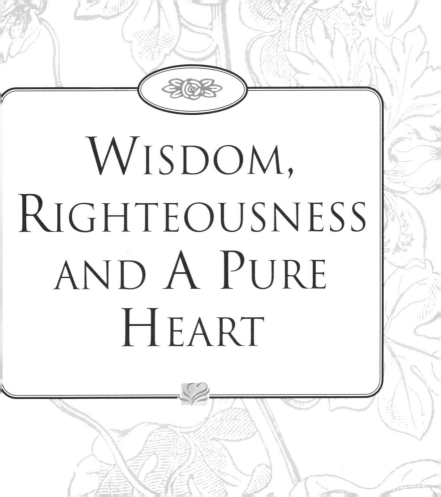

WISDOM, RIGHTEOUSNESS AND A PURE HEART

$\mathcal{G}$et wisdom, get understanding; do not forget my words or swerve from them. Do not forsake wisdom, and she will protect you; love her, and she will watch over you. Wisdom is supreme; therefore get wisdom. Though it cost all you have, get understanding. Esteem her, and she will exalt you; embrace her, and she will honor you.

Proverbs 4:5–8

$\mathcal{T}$rust in the LORD with all your heart and lean not on your own understanding; in all your ways acknowledge him, and he will make your paths straight. Do not be wise in your own eyes; fear the LORD and shun evil. This will bring health to your body and nourishment to your bones.

Proverbs 3:5–8

*H*appy are those who find wisdom, and those who get understanding, for her income is better than silver, and her revenue better than gold. She is more precious than jewels, and nothing you desire can compare with her. Long life is in her right hand; in her left hand are riches and honor. Her ways are ways of pleasantness, and all her paths are peace. She is a tree of life to those who lay hold of her; those who hold her fast are called happy.

Proverbs 3:13-18 (NRSV)

$\mathcal{N}$ow then, my sons, listen to me; blessed are those who keep my ways. Listen to my instruction and be wise; do not ignore it. Blessed is the man who listens to me. For whoever finds me finds life and receives favor from the LORD.

Proverbs 8:32–35

$\mathcal{F}$or surely, O LORD, you bless the righteous; you surround them with your favor as with a shield.

Psalm 5:12

*R*ejoice in the LORD and be glad, you righteous;
sing, all you who are upright in heart!

Psalm 32:11

*S*ing joyfully to the LORD, you righteous;
it is fitting for the upright to praise him. Praise
the LORD with the harp; make music to him
on the ten-stringed lyre.

Psalm 33:1–2

*B*lessed is the man whose sin the LORD does not
count against him and in whose spirit is no deceit.

Psalm 32:2

*H*e who has clean hands and a pure heart, who does not lift up his soul to an idol or swear by what is false. He will receive blessing from the LORD and vindication from God his Savior.

Psalm 24:4–5

❧

*C*reate in me a pure heart, O God, and renew a steadfast spirit within me. Restore to me the joy of your salvation and grant me a willing spirit, to sustain me.

Psalm 51:10,12

$\mathscr{B}$lessed are all who fear the LORD, who walk in his ways. You will eat the fruit of your labor; blessings and prosperity will be yours. . . . Thus is the man blessed who fears the LORD.

Psalm 128:1–2,4

❧

$\mathscr{T}$he LORD loves righteousness and justice; the earth is full of his unfailing love.

Psalm 33:5

GOD'S PLAN AND HIS PURPOSE

*F*or I know the plans I have for you, declares the
LORD, plans to prosper you and not to harm you,
plans to give you hope and a future.

Jeremiah 29:11

❧

*C*ommit to the LORD whatever you do,
and your plans will succeed.

Proverbs 16:3

$\mathcal{G}$ood and upright is the LORD. He guides the humble in what is right and teaches them his way.

Psalm 25:8–9

❧

$\mathcal{F}$or this God is our God for ever and ever; he will be our guide even to the end.

Psalm 48:14

*B*ut the plans of the LORD stand firm forever, the purposes of his heart through all generations.

Psalm 33:11

❧

*T*rust in the LORD and do good; dwell in the land and enjoy safe pasture. Delight yourself in the LORD and he will give you the desires of your heart.

Psalm 37:3–4

*F*or God remembered his holy promise given to his servant Abraham. He brought out his people with rejoicing, his chosen ones with shouts of joy; he gave them the lands of the nations, and they fell heir to what others had toiled for— that they might keep his precepts and observe his laws. Praise the LORD.

Psalm 105:42–45

*A*nd the ransomed of the LORD will return. They will enter Zion with singing; everlasting joy will crown their heads. Gladness and joy will overtake them, and sorrow and sighing will flee away.

Isaiah 35:10

❧

*T*he Lord is not slow in keeping his promise, as some understand slowness. He is patient with you, not wanting anyone to perish, but everyone to come to repentance.

2 Peter 3:9

OUR SAVIOR AND SALVATION

*T*he LORD is my strength and my song; he has become my salvation. He is my God, and I will praise him, my father's God, and I will exalt him.

Exodus 15:2

*R*ejoice greatly, O Daughter of Zion! Shout, Daughter of Jerusalem! See, your king comes to you, righteous and having salvation, gentle and riding on a donkey, on a colt, the foal of a donkey.

Zechariah 9:9

$\mathscr{T}$he LORD is good to those whose hope is in him,
to the one who seeks him; it is good to wait quietly
for the salvation of the LORD.

Lamentations 3:25–26

$\mathscr{T}$he angel said to them, "Do not be afraid. I bring
you good news of great joy that will be for all the
people. Today in the town of David a Savior has
been born to you; he is Christ the Lord."

Luke 2:10–11

$\mathcal{A}$s the Father has loved me, so have I loved you. Now remain in my love. If you obey my commands, you will remain in my love, just as I have obeyed my Father's commands and remain in his love. I have told you this so that my joy may be in you and that your joy may be complete.

John 15:9–11

*U*ntil now you have not asked for anything
in my name. Ask and you will receive,
and your joy will be complete.

John 16:24

❧

*S*how me your ways, O LORD, teach me your paths;
guide me in your truth and teach me, for you are
God my Savior, and my hope is in you all day long.

Psalm 25:4

$\mathcal{Y}$ou will seek me and find me when you seek me with all your heart, says the LORD.

Jeremiah 29:13

❧

$\mathcal{T}$he LORD lives! Praise be to my Rock! Exalted be God, the Rock, my Savior!

2 Samuel 22:47

*C*leanse me with hyssop, and I will be clean;
wash me, and I will be whiter than snow.
Let me hear joy and gladness; let the bones
you have crushed rejoice.

Psalm 51:7–8

*F*or God so loved the world that he gave his one and only Son, that whoever believes in him shall not perish but have eternal life. For God did not send his Son into the world to condemn the world, but to save the world through him.

John 3:16–17

$\mathscr{P}$raise the LORD, O my soul; all my inmost
being, praise his holy name. Praise the LORD,
O my soul, and forget not all his benefits—who
forgives all your sins and heals all your diseases,
who redeems your life from the pit and crowns
you with love and compassion, who satisfies your
desires with good things so that your youth is
renewed like the eagle's.

Psalm 103:1–5

*B*ut as for me, I watch in hope for the LORD, I wait for God my Savior; my God will hear me.

Micah 7:7

❧

*F*rom the LORD comes deliverance. May your blessing be on your people.

Psalm 3:8

$\mathcal{B}$ut I trust in your unfailing love; my heart rejoices in your salvation. I will sing to the LORD, for he has been good to me.

Psalm 13:5–6

$\mathcal{H}$appy are those whose transgression is forgiven, whose sin is covered. Happy are those to whom the LORD imputes no iniquity, and in whose spirit there is no deceit.

Psalm 32:1–2 (NRSV)

*R*emember me, O LORD, when you show favor to your people, come to my aid when you save them, that I may enjoy the prosperity of your chosen ones, that I may share in the joy of your nation and join your inheritance in giving praise.

Psalm 106:4–5

❧

*F*or the LORD takes delight in his people; he crowns the humble with salvation. Let the saints rejoice in this honor and sing for joy.

Psalm 149:4–5

*C*ome, let us sing for joy to the LORD; let us shout aloud to the Rock of our salvation. Let us come before him with thanksgiving and extol him with music and song. For the LORD is the great God, the great King above all gods.

Psalm 95:1–3

*S*urely God is my salvation; I will trust and not be afraid. The LORD, the LORD, is my strength and my song; he has become my salvation.

Isaiah 12:2

❧

*G*od will be the sure foundation for your times, a rich store of salvation and wisdom and knowledge; the fear of the LORD is the key to this treasure.

Isaiah 33:6

I delight greatly in the L ORD; my soul rejoices in my God. For he has clothed me with garments of salvation and arrayed me in a robe of righteousness, as a bridegroom adorns his head like a priest, and as a bride adorns herself with her jewels.

Isaiah 61:10

I tell you that there will be more rejoicing
in heaven over one sinner who repents
than over ninety-nine righteous persons
who do not need to repent.

Luke 15:7

*T*hough you have not seen Jesus Christ,
you love him; and even though you do not see
him now, you believe in him and are filled with
an inexpressible and glorious joy, for you
are receiving the goal of your faith, the
salvation of your souls.

1 Peter 1:8–9

GOD'S PROVISION AND PROTECTION

$\mathcal{H}$e makes grass grow for the cattle, and plants for man to cultivate—bringing forth food from the earth: wine that gladdens the heart of man, oil to make his face shine, and bread that sustains his heart.

Psalm 104:14–15

$\mathcal{Y}$et God has not left himself without testimony: He has shown kindness by giving you rain from heaven and crops in their seasons; he provides you with plenty of food and fills your hearts with joy.

Acts 14:17

$\mathcal{T}$o the One who remembered us in our low estate, his love endures forever. Who freed us from our enemies, his love endures forever. And who gives food to every creature, his love endures forever. Give thanks to the God of heaven, his love endures forever.

Psalm 136:23–26

*T*he eyes of all look to you, O L<small>ORD</small>, and you give them their food at the proper time. You open your hand and satisfy the desires of every living thing.

Psalm 145:15–16

✑

*M*y mouth will speak in praise of the L<small>ORD</small>.
Let every creature praise his holy name
for ever and ever.

Psalm 145:21

*C*ommand those who are rich in this present world not to be arrogant nor to put their hope in wealth, which is so uncertain, but to put their hope in God, who richly provides us with everything for our enjoyment.

1 Timothy 6:17

You have filled my heart with greater joy
than when grain and new wine abound. I will
lie down and sleep in peace, for you alone,
O LORD, make me dwell in safety.

Psalm 4:7–8

You, O LORD, are my hiding place; you
will protect me from trouble and surround
me with songs of deliverance.

Psalm 32:7

$\mathscr{B}$ut let all who take refuge in you, O God,
be glad; let them ever sing for joy. Spread your
protection over them, that those who love
your name may rejoice in you.

Psalm 5:11

"Because he loves me," says the LORD,
"I will rescue him; I will protect him, for
he acknowledges my name."

Psalm 91:14

*H*appy are those who consider the poor;
the LORD delivers them in the day of trouble.
The LORD protects them and keeps them alive;
they are called happy in the land. You do
not give them up to the will of their enemies.
The LORD sustains them on their sickbed;
in their illness you heal all their infirmities.

Psalm 41:1–3 (NRSV)

I love you, O LORD, my strength. The LORD
is my rock, my fortress and my deliverer; my God
is my rock, in whom I take refuge. He is my shield
and the horn of my salvation, my stronghold.
I call to the LORD, who is worthy of praise, and
I am saved from my enemies.

Psalm 18:1–3

❧

T he LORD is my strength and my shield; my heart
trusts in him, and I am helped. My heart leaps for
joy and I will give thanks to him in song.

Psalm 28:7

*B*ut I will sing of your strength, in the morning I will sing of your love; for you are my fortress, my refuge in times of trouble. O my Strength, I sing praise to you; you, O God, are my fortress, my loving God.

Psalm 59:16–17

*L*et the righteous rejoice in the LORD and take refuge in him; let all the upright in heart praise him!

Psalm 64:10

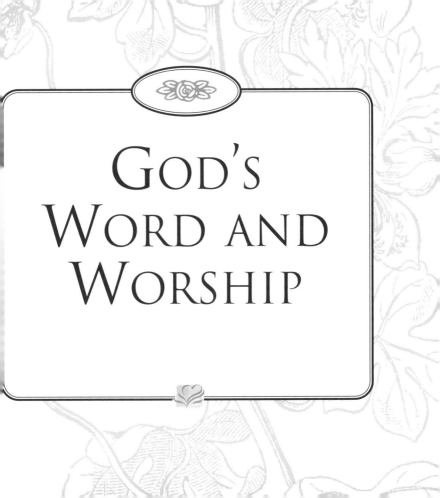

GOD'S
WORD AND
WORSHIP

*H*appy are those who do not follow the advice of the wicked, or take the path that sinners tread, or sit in the seat of scoffers; but their delight is in the law of the LORD, and on his law they meditate day and night. They are like trees planted by streams of water, which yield their fruit in its season, and their leaves do not wither. In all that they do, they prosper.

Psalm 1:1–3 (NRSV)

*S*ing to him a new song. For the word of the LORD is right and true; he is faithful in all he does. The LORD loves righteousness and justice; the earth is full of his unfailing love.

Psalm 33:3–5

❧

*Y*our word is a lamp to my feet
and a light for my path.
Psalm 119:105

❧

*Y*our word, O Lord, is eternal; it stands
firm in the heavens.
Psalm 119:89

I have not departed from the commands
of his lips; I have treasured the words of his
mouth more than my daily bread.

Job 23:12

❧

*W*hen your words came, they were my
joy and my heart's delight, for I bear your
name, O Lord God Almighty.

Jeremiah 15:16

*W*orship the LORD your God; it is he who will deliver you from the hand of all your enemies.

2 Kings 17:39

❧

*P*raise the LORD. Blessed is the man who fears the LORD, who finds great delight in his commands. His children will be mighty in the land; the generation of the upright will be blessed.

Psalm 112:1–2

I rejoice in following your statutes, O God, as one rejoices in great riches. I meditate on your precepts and consider your ways. I delight in your decrees; I will not neglect your word.

Psalm 119:14–16

❧

*I*n my inner being I delight in God's law.

Romans 7:22

*Y*our statutes are my heritage forever;
they are the joy of my heart.

Psalm 119:111

❧

I rejoice in your promise, O God, like one
who finds great spoil.

Psalm 119:162

❧

*M*ay my lips overflow with praise, O LORD,
for you teach me your decrees.

Psalm 119:171

As the rain and the snow come down from heaven, and do not return to it without watering the earth and making it bud and flourish, so that it yields seed for the sower and bread for the eater, so is my word that goes out from my mouth: It will not return to me empty, but will accomplish what I desire and achieve the purpose for which I sent it.

Isaiah 55:10–11

$\mathscr{K}$eep his decrees and commands, which
I am giving you today, so that it may go well
with you and your children after you and
that you may live long in the land the LORD
your God gives you for all time.

Dueteronomy 4:40

$\mathscr{F}$or everything that was written in the past
was written to teach us, so that through
endurance and the encouragement of the
Scriptures we might have hope.

Romans 15:4

One thing I ask of the LORD, this is what I seek: that I may dwell in the house of the LORD all the days of my life, to gaze upon the beauty of the LORD and to seek him in his temple.

Psalm 27:4

For in the day of trouble he will keep me
safe in his dwelling; he will hide me in the shelter
of his tabernacle and set me high upon a rock.
Then my head will be exalted above the
enemies who surround me; at his tabernacle
will I sacrifice with shouts of joy; I will sing
and make music to the LORD.

Psalm 27:5-6

*Y*ou turned my wailing into dancing; you removed my sackcloth and clothed me with joy, that my heart may sing to you and not be silent. O LORD my God, I will give you thanks forever.

Psalm 30:11–12

❧

*B*ut may the righteous be glad and rejoice before God; may they be happy and joyful. Sing to God, sing praise to his name, extol him who rides on the clouds—his name is the LORD— and rejoice before him.

Psalm 68:3–4

*I*n the beginning was the Word, and the Word
was with God, and the Word was God.

John 1:1

❧

*A*s for God, his way is perfect; the word
of the LORD is flawless. He is a shield for all
who take refuge in him.

2 Samuel 22:31

$\mathcal{I}$t is good to praise the LORD and make music to your name, O Most High, to proclaim your love in the morning and your faithfulness at night, to the music of the ten-stringed lyre and the melody of the harp.

Psalm 92:1–3

$\mathscr{I}$will extol the LORD at all times; his praise will always be on my lips. My soul will boast in the LORD; let the afflicted hear and rejoice. Glorify the LORD with me; let us exalt his name together.

Psalm 34:1–3

I will sing to the LORD all my life; I will
sing praise to my God as long as I live.
May my meditation be pleasing to him,
as I rejoice in the LORD.

Psalm 104:33–34

❧

S hout for joy to the LORD, all the earth.
Worship the LORD with gladness; come
before him with joyful songs.

Psalm 100:1

❧

I rejoiced with those who said to me, "Let us go
to the house of the LORD."

Psalm 122:1

$\mathscr{P}$raise the LORD. Sing to the LORD a new song,
his praise in the assembly of the saints.
Let Israel rejoice in their Maker; let the people
of Zion be glad in their King. Let them praise
his name with dancing and make music to him
with tambourine and harp.

Psalm 149:1–3

GOD'S
COMFORT AND
UNFAILING
LOVE

$\mathcal{S}$hout for joy, O heavens; rejoice, O earth;
burst into song, O mountains! For the LORD
comforts his people and will have compassion
on his afflicted ones.

Isaiah 49:13

$\mathcal{T}$his is what the LORD says, "As a mother
comforts her child, so will I comfort you; and you
will be comforted over Jerusalem." When you see
this, your heart will rejoice and you will flourish
like grass; the hand of the LORD will be made
known to his servants.

Isaiah 66:13

$\mathcal{Y}$ou will increase my honor and comfort me once again. I will praise you with the harp for your faithfulness, O my God; I will sing praise to you with the lyre, O Holy One of Israel.

Psalm 71:21–22

$\mathcal{H}$e who dwells in the shelter of the Most High will rest in the shadow of the Almighty. I will say of the LORD, "He is my refuge and my fortress, my God, in whom I trust."

Psalm 91:1–2

*T*he Spirit of the Sovereign LORD is on me, and he has sent me to bind up the brokenhearted, to proclaim freedom for the captives and release from darkness for the prisoners, to proclaim the year of the LORD's favor, to comfort all who mourn, and provide for those who grieve—to bestow on them a crown of beauty instead of ashes, the oil of gladness instead of mourning, and a garment of praise instead of a spirit of despair. They will be called oaks of righteousness, a planting of the LORD for the display of his splendor.

Isaiah 61:1–3

*E*ven though I walk through the valley
of the shadow of death, I will fear no evil,
for you are with me; your rod and your staff,
they comfort me.

Psalm 23:4

"*I* will turn their mourning into gladness;
I will give them comfort and joy instead of
sorrow," says the Lord.
Jeremiah 31:13

❧

*R*eturn to the Lord your God, for he is gracious
and compassionate, slow to anger and abounding
in love, and he relents from sending calamity.
Joel 2:13

$\mathcal{P}$raise be to the God and Father of our Lord Jesus Christ, the Father of compassion and the God of all comfort, who comforts us in all our troubles, so that we can comfort those in any trouble with the comfort we ourselves have received from God.

2 Corinthians 1:3–4

$\mathcal{Y}$et this I call to mind and therefore I have hope:
Because of the LORD's great love we are not
consumed, for his compassions never fail. They are
new every morning; great is your faithfulness.

Lamentations 3:21–23

❧

$\mathcal{S}$atisfy us in the morning with your unfailing love,
that we may sing for joy and be glad all our days.

Psalm 90:14

$\mathcal{I}$will praise you, O Lord, among the nations;
I will sing of you among the peoples. For great
is your love, reaching to the heavens; your
faithfulness reaches to the skies.

Psalm 57:9–10

$\mathcal{P}$raise the LORD, all you nations; extol him,
all you peoples. For great is his love toward us,
and the faithfulness of the LORD endures
forever. Praise the LORD.

Psalm 117:1–2

*P*raise the LORD. Give thanks to the LORD, for he is good; his love endures forever.

Psalm 106:1

❧

*L*et them give thanks to the LORD for his unfailing love and his wonderful deeds for men, for he satisfies the thirsty and fills the hungry with good things.

Psalm 107:8–9

*I*call on you, O God, for you will answer me; give ear to me and hear my prayer. Show the wonder of your great love, you who save by your right hand those who take refuge in you from their foes.

Psalm 17:6-7

❧

*M*any are the torments of the wicked, but steadfast love surrounds those who trust in the LORD. Be glad in the LORD and rejoice, O righteous, and shout for joy, all you upright in heart.

Psalm 32:10–11 (NRSV)

*H*e will wipe every tear from their eyes.
There will be no more death or mourning or
crying or pain, for the old order of things has
passed away. He who was seated on the throne
said, "I am making everything new!" Then he
said, "Write this down, for these words are
trustworthy and true."
Revelation 21:4–5

*I*n him our hearts rejoice, for we trust in his
holy name. May your unfailing love rest upon us,
O LORD, even as we put our hope in you.

Psalm 33:21–22

❧

*B*ecause your love is better than life,
my lips will glorify you.

Psalm 63:3

*P*raise be to God, who has not rejected
my prayer or withheld his love from me!
Psalm 66:20

❧

*B*ut may all who seek you rejoice and be glad
in you; may those who love your salvation
always say, "Let God be exalted!"
Psalm 70:4

$\mathcal{G}$ive thanks to the LORD, for he is good,
his love endures forever. Give thanks to the God
of gods, his love endures forever. Give thanks
to the Lord of lords: his love endures forever.
To him who alone does great wonders,
his love endures forever.

Psalm 136:1-4

*W*ho by his understanding made the heavens, his love endures forever. Who spread out the earth upon the waters, his love endures forever. Who made the great lights—his love endures forever. The sun to govern the day, his love endures forever. The moon and stars to govern the night; his love endures forever.

Psalm 136:5-9

*I*t is good to praise the LORD and make music to your name, O Most High, to proclaim your love in the morning and your faithfulness at night.

Psalm 92:1–2

❧

*E*nter his gates with thanksgiving and his courts with praise; give thanks to him and praise his name. For the LORD is good and his love endures forever; his faithfulness continues through all generations.

Psalm 100:4–5

I will bow down toward your holy temple
and will praise your name for your love and
your faithfulness, for you have exalted above
all things your name and your word.

Psalm 138:2

*B*ut from everlasting to everlasting the LORD's
love is with those who fear him, and his
righteousness with their children's children.

Psalm 103:17

*W*ill you not revive us again, that your people
may rejoice in you? Show us your unfailing love,
O LORD, and grant us your salvation.

Psalm 85:6–7

❧

*L*et them give thanks to the LORD for his
unfailing love and his wonderful deeds for men.
Let them tell of his works with songs of joy.

Psalm 107:21–22

"*Though* the mountains be shaken and the hills be removed, yet my unfailing love for you will not be shaken nor my covenant of peace be removed," says the LORD, who has compassion on you.

Isaiah 54:10

❧

Not to us, O LORD, not to us but to your name be the glory, because of your love and faithfulness.

Psalm 115:1

*M*y heart is steadfast, O God; I will sing and make music with all my soul. Awake, harp and lyre! I will awaken the dawn. I will praise you, O LORD, among the nations; I will sing of you among the peoples. For great is your love, higher than the heavens; your faithfulness reaches to the skies. Be exalted, O God, above the heavens, and let your glory be over all the earth.

Psalm 108:1–5

I will praise you, O Lord my God, with all my heart; I will glorify your name forever. For great is your love toward me.

Psalm 86:12–13

❧

I will sing of the Lord's great love forever; with my mouth I will make your faithfulness known through all generations. I will declare that your love stands firm forever, that you established your faithfulness in heaven itself.

Psalm 89:1–2

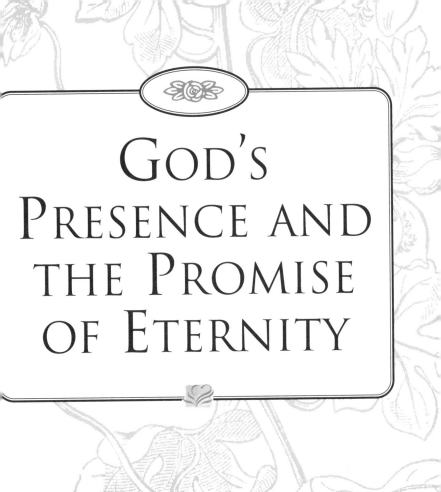

GOD'S PRESENCE AND THE PROMISE OF ETERNITY

*Y*ou have made known to me the path of life;
you will fill me with joy in your presence, with
eternal pleasures at your right hand.

Psalm 16:11

*S*urely you have granted him eternal blessings
and made him glad with the joy of your presence.

Psalm 21:6

*W*here can I go from your Spirit? Where can I flee from your presence? If I go up to the heavens, you are there; if I make my bed in the depths, you are there. If I rise on the wings of the dawn, if I settle on the far side of the sea, even there your hand will guide me, your right hand will hold me fast.

Psalm 139:7-10

❧

*B*lessed are those who have learned to acclaim you, who walk in the light of your presence, O LORD. They rejoice in your name all day long; they exult in your righteousness.

Psalm 89:15–16

*W*ith what shall I come before the LORD and bow down before the exalted God?... He has showed you, O man, what is good. And what does the LORD require of you? To act justly and to love mercy and to walk humbly with your God.

Micah 6:6, 8

❧

*M*ay he strengthen your hearts so that you will be blameless and holy in the presence of our God and Father when our Lord Jesus comes with all his holy ones.

1 Thessalonians 3:13

I tell you the truth, whoever hears my word and believes him who sent me has eternal life and will not be condemned; he has crossed over from death to life.

John 5:24

❧

I give them eternal life, and they shall never perish; no one can snatch them out of my hand. My Father, who has given them to me, is greater than all; no one can snatch them out of my Father's hand. I and the Father are one.

John 10:28-30

*I*nstead of their shame my people will receive a double portion, and instead of disgrace they will rejoice in their inheritance; and so they will inherit a double portion in their land, and everlasting joy will be theirs.

Isaiah 61:7

*R*ejoice in that day and leap for joy, because great is your reward in heaven.

Luke 6:23

❧

*J*esus said, "Now is your time of grief, but I will see you again and you will rejoice, and no one will take away your joy."

John 16:22

$\mathscr{F}$or our light and momentary troubles are achieving for us an eternal glory that far outweighs them all. So we fix our eyes not on what is seen, but on what is unseen. For what is seen is temporary, but what is unseen is eternal.

2 Corinthians 4:17–18

*P*raise be to the God and Father of our Lord Jesus Christ! In his great mercy he has given us new birth into a living hope through the resurrection of Jesus Christ from the dead, and into an inheritance that can never perish, spoil or fade—kept in heaven.

1 Peter 1:3–4

❧

*L*et us fix our eyes on Jesus, the author and perfecter of our faith, who for the joy set before him endured the cross, scorning its shame, and sat down at the right hand of the throne of God.

Hebrews 12:2

❧

*L*et us rejoice and be glad and give him glory! For the wedding of the Lamb has come, and his bride has made herself ready.

Revelation 19:7